High Interest/Low Readability

Inventions

Published by Milestone
an imprint of
Frank Schaffer Publications®

Author: Delana Heidrich
Editors: Linda Triemstra, Raymond Wiersma

Frank Schaffer Publications®

Milestone is an imprint of Frank Schaffer Publications.

Send all inquiries to:
Frank Schaffer Publications
8720 Orion Place
Columbus, Ohio 43240-2111

High Interest/Low Readability, Inventions

ISBN: 0-7696-3395-1

2 3 4 5 6 7 8 9 10 MAZ 11 10 09 08 07

Table of Contents

Introduction

If necessity is the mother of invention, error is the father. Countless foods we eat, products we purchase, and machines we operate owe their existence to lab mistakes, chance occurrences, and freak accidents. If a political cartoon had not illustrated a bear cub's encounter with President Theodore Roosevelt on a hunting trip, children may never have called their stuffed bears "Teddy." Should Mrs. Josephine Dickson not have been so accident-prone, her husband may never have invented a do-it-yourself bandage. Had a war economy not have required the nation to find substitutes for rubber, consumers may never have experienced the joy of stretching, smashing, and bouncing Silly Putty®.

Fascinating stories of chance and error lie behind the inventions of doughnut holes, chewing gum, jeans, and more. *High Interest/Low Readability, Inventions* contains eight intriguing tales of inventions of chance and error. Each story is preceded by prereading activities and followed by comprehension and follow-up activities. Use these eight complete lessons to motivate and encourage your students while providing them practice at the skills needed to read for meaning, insight, and enjoyment.

Nature Inspires: Teddy Bears and Velcro® Fasteners • By-Products of War: Silly Putty® and the Slinky® • Making Great Strides: Improvements in Doughnuts and Rubber

Zip and Chip: Step-by-Step Inventions • Inventions by Chance: Chewing Gum and Ice Cream • Naismith Ball: The Birth of a New Sport

What to Do with It: The Inventions of Jeans and Post-it® Notes • Clean It Off and Bandage It: The Inventions of Ivory® Soap and Band-Aids®

Name _____ Date _____

Prereading Activities

Looking It Over

1. Read the title of the article that begins on page 6.

2. Leaf through the pages of the article, stopping to look at the pictures.

3. Read the list of vocabulary words.

What Do You Know?

List some of the uses of Post-it® Notes.

_____

_____

When do people wear jeans? What age group wears jeans for fashion? What workers wear jeans in their occupations?

_____

_____

Make a Prediction

Consider the title of the article. What might the inventions of sticky notes and jeans have in common?

_____

_____

_____

_____

Read the article to increase your knowledge.

Vocabulary

trousers   pants

Example: Miners needed sturdy trousers for the hard work of searching for gold.

generation   a single step in descent or progress

Example: The first generation of jeans was brown.

bolts   rolls of cloth

Example: Levi Strauss bought bolts and bolts of denim to make his jeans.

rivets   metal pin-and-nut fasteners

Example: Rivets added to stress points make jeans sturdy.

garment   clothing

Example: A flowered skirt is my favorite garment.

concocted   prepared, mixed, created

Example: Spence Silver concocted a new strength of glue.

What to Do with It: The Inventions of Jeans and Post-it® Notes

Spence Silver, Art Fry, and Levi Strauss had a similar problem: what to do with a seemingly useless product.

Tent Canvas Turned Overalls

In 1848, gold was found at Sutter's Mill. The gold rush was on. Twenty-three-year-old Levi Strauss joined the rush. But he didn't hope to find gold. He hoped to sell supplies to the men and women who did. So Strauss moved to San Francisco. He set up a store and ran an honest business. He became rich and well respected.

0-7696-3395-1 *Inventions*

One day Strauss bought denim canvas to sell at his store. He thought miners would cover their wagons and build tents with it. But they didn't. California's weather was nice. Miners slept directly under the stars. Strauss would have to find another use for his yards and yards of canvas. One of his customers said Strauss should try to make a sturdy pair of trousers with his canvas. Miners needed strong pants. Strauss listened to his customer. The first generation of jeans was born. They were called "waist overalls."

One day Strauss talked with a man named Jacob Davis. Davis was a tailor who often brought bolts of cloth to Strauss's store. Davis had come up with a way to strengthen trousers. He placed metal rivets at pocket corners and the base of the fly. But he did not have the money to patent his idea. Strauss paid for the paperwork. The two men applied for a patent together. The second generation of jeans was born. Eventually, new fabrics were used in jeans. The term *jeans* was born out of the name of a city in Italy where some of this new fabric came from.

Levi jeans did not change the life of Strauss much. He was already a rich man. The jeans did change the lives of the rest of us. In fact, the Levi Company says jeans are the only garment invented in the nineteenth century that is still worn today.

Personal Bookmark = Big Business

Early in the 1970s, Dr. Spence Silver concocted a glue. It was strong enough to stick papers together. It wasn't strong enough to hold. Dr. Silver had no use for his glue. Art Fry did.

Fry worked with Silver. He knew all about his strange glue. He asked his friend if he could use some of the stuff. Fry smeared the glue on strips of paper. He took the paper strips to church. He placed one strip on the page of each of the hymns he would sing in choir that day. That way he could turn to the correct page quickly.

Silver's glue was useful to Fry. But it may never have made it out of the choir loft if Fry didn't use it in the office one day as well. He jotted an idea on one of the glued strips of paper. When he stuck the paper to a report, Fry realized something. The glued paper could be useful for more than just bookmarks. It could be used to attach notes to reports. Silver's new glue now had a marketable use. Or so it seemed.

It took Fry's team 18 months to develop Post-it® Notes. Then they were ready to sell. At first, the notes were marketed in four large cities. Maybe Fry was the only man who saw their usefulness. The notes did not sell.

The 3M Corporation was not ready to give up on its new product. It sent two men out to sell it face to face. They showed uses for the notes in offices all over Richmond, California. When offices placed orders there, the men moved on. They sold the product in Boise, Idaho. The demonstrations and free samples were successful there, too. They went on to 11 more states. Sample states began ordering sticky notes for themselves. They also made orders for their branches in nonsample states. By 1980, the lightly glued papers were available in all 50 states. By the following year they were for sale in Canada and Europe, too.

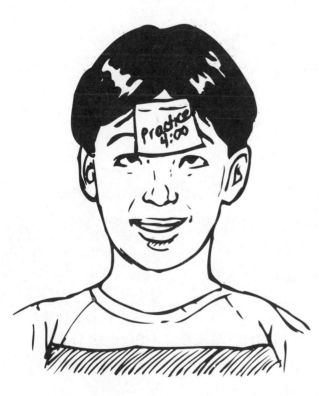

Today, many Post-it® products are sold. The original notes can be bought in many sizes and colors. Electronic notes can be used on the Internet. Signs have been devised for temporary use such as bake sales. Memo boards make updating information easy. Easel pads make public speaking easy. Fry's bookmark idea has evolved into big business for the 3M Corporation.

Comprehension

Circle the best answer. Highlight the sentence or sentences in the story where you find each answer.

1. What do the inventions of jeans and Post-it® Notes have in common?
   a. They were both invented in the late 1900s.
   b. They were both invented by a woman.
   c. They were both intended to be used by miners.
   d. They both made use of a material that was readily available to their inventors.

2. Who suggested Strauss create sturdy pants for miners?
   a. his wife
   b. his mother
   c. one of his customers
   d. his boss

3. Levi Strauss went to California because . . .
   a. he hoped to sell supplies to gold miners.
   b. he hoped to find gold.
   c. his family lived in San Francisco.
   d. he didn't like winter weather.

4. Strauss's jeans didn't change his life much because . . .
   a. Jacob Davis made all the money off the invention.
   b. he was already a rich man.
   c. he died before jeans began to sell.
   d. they never sold well.

5. Gold rushers did not buy tent canvas because . . .
   a. they brought tents with them from the East Coast.
   b. they slept in their covered wagons.
   c. canvas was not waterproof.
   d. warm weather allowed them to sleep without tents.

Name _____ Date _____

6. Who invented the glue used in Post-it® Notes?
   a. Art Fry
   b. Spence Silver
   c. Levi Strauss
   d. Richmond Jones

7. Which statement about Post-it® Notes is true?
   a. They were invented by one man.
   b. It took a team of workers 18 months to develop them.
   c. They were a big seller from the beginning.
   d. They were first sold as bookmarks at book stores.

8. Art Fry first used his friend's glue to . . .
   a. place strips of paper on the pages of his church hymnal.
   b. seal envelopes.
   c. stick a grocery list to his refrigerator.
   d. stick notes onto his computer.

9. Today, Spence Silver's glue is not used on . . .
   a. easel pads.
   b. temporary signs.
   c. memo boards.
   d. shirt pocket flaps.

10. Post-it® Notes sold well after . . .
   a. samples were mailed to music stores.
   b. 3M Corporation employees demonstrated the use of the product in person.
   c. a famous television ad popularized the product.
   d. magazines began advertising the product.

What to Do with It: The Inventions of Jeans and Post-it® Notes

Discussion Questions

1. Describe the processes that jeans and Post-it® Notes went through to become marketable.

2. The employees at the 3M Corporation work as members of a team. When given the choice, do you like to complete classroom assignments alone or in a group? What are the advantages and disadvantages of each way of working?

3. If you were Levi Strauss and you heard about the gold rush, would you move to California to dig for gold or to open a store? Why?

Step by Step

The invention and sale of Post-it® Notes was a team effort. Fill in the steps taken along the way. Some steps have been recorded for you.

1. _____

2. Art Fry uses the new glue at church.

3. _____

4. Fry's team develops Post-it® Notes in 18 months.

5. _____

6. _____

Vocabulary Activities

Which word from the Word Bank comes to mind as you read each sentence below? Record your responses in the spaces provided.

> **Word Bank**
> | generation | bolts | rivets |
> | trousers | garments | concocted |

_____ 1. Spence Silver cooked up a batch of glue.

_____ 2. A family reunion includes people of all ages.

_____ 3. Levi Strauss needed lots of fabric.

_____ 4. My suitcase is filled with pants, shirts, skirts, and dresses.

_____ 5. Little metal circles at stress points can make jeans stronger.

_____ 6. Gold diggers needed sturdy pants.

Homework

Write a letter to the Levi Strauss company commenting on their product.

Extension

Research and report on the history of American fashion.

Prereading Activities

Looking It Over

1. Read the title of the article that begins on page 16.
2. Leaf through the pages of the article, stopping to look at the pictures.
3. Read the list of vocabulary words.

What Do You Know?

Record here all you know about the history of soap and first aid.

_____

_____

Make a Prediction

Why do you think Ivory® Soap floats?

_____

_____

_____

_____

How do you think people cared for minor wounds before the invention of adhesive bandages?

_____

_____

_____

_____

Read the article to add to your knowledge.

Vocabulary

oversight   something that went unnoticed accidentally

Example: The fact that you did not get your report card was an oversight on my part.

adhesive   having the ability to stick

Example: Adhesive bandages stay on to your skin.

cleansers   cleaning products

Example: You'll need lots of cleansers to get this kitchen clean!

vogue   fashionable, popular

Example: Frequent bathing was not in vogue until the late 1800s.

froth   foam and bubbles

Example: My root beer float had froth on top.

bandages   gauze used to cover wounds

Example: Before bandages were adhesive, they were stuck to the skin with medical tape.

doggedly   stubbornly

Example: I studied doggedly for my math final and passed it with a B.

Clean It Off and Bandage It: The Inventions of Ivory Soap® and Band-Aids®

Ivory® Soap and Band-Aids® have something in common. They were both inventions of chance. A soap maker's oversight brought us Ivory® Soap. An accident-prone housewife inspired the creation of Band-Aids®.

All Washed Up

Soap has been around a long time. Cleansers are mentioned in the Bible. Five-thousand-year-old clay tablets have soap recipes. Soap dyes are referred to in first-century A.D. writings.

Yet soap was not used much at first. Early people bathed only twice a year. Even then, they didn't always use soap. It was thought to take too many oils out of the skin. Soap was thought good only for cleaning wounds then.

By 1878, bathing was at last in vogue. So was soap. Soap making in America was big business. Companies fought for a corner of the market. In that year, James N. Gamble came up with a white soap. He was very proud of it. Other soaps then were a dingy gray.

0-7696-3395-1 Inventions

Gamble headed the Procter and Gamble Company. He thought he would name his new soap P&G soap. Mr. Proctor thought of a better name. He heard the words "out of the ivory palaces" read in church one Sunday. He said the white soap should be called "Ivory." The name sounded white. It sounded pure. Gamble liked it. In 1879, the first bar of Ivory® Soap was sold.

Then the accident occurred. A batch of soap was cooking. It was lunch time at the factory. The soap cooker forgot to turn off the machine. By the time he returned, the soap batch had cooked too long. It looked frothy. Still, he packaged the soap. It was shipped out as usual. People liked the mistake. They asked for more of the "floating soap." What started out as an accident became a big hit. "It floats"™ became an Ivory® slogan in 1891.

Today, soap makers could not make the same mistake. The machines are too advanced to ruin a single batch of suds. The makers of Ivory® whip extra air into their soap on purpose now. Sometimes we strive doggedly toward success. Sometimes we stumble onto it!

Do-It-Yourself Bandages

Adhesive bandages are taken for granted today. Yet they have not been around that long. Before 1920, it was not easy to cover a cut or scrape. First, gauze was cut. Then, it was folded to fit the wound. Next, tape was cut from a long, sticky roll. It was placed over the gauze. The whole process was hard to manage with one hand. And Josephine Dickson had to go through the process often.

Dickson was the young bride of Earle. Earle worked for the Johnson and Johnson Company. He worked at the office. Josephine cooked and cleaned at home. Alas, she was accident-prone in the kitchen. Along with the carrots, she sliced into her own fingers. Along with the roast beef, she burned her own hands. Caring for her wounds was hard with one hand. More than once, she had to wait for Earle to get home to get bandaged up just right.

Earle thought there must be a way to turn treating a wound into a one-person job. He unrolled a long piece of tape. He placed a folded piece of gauze every few inches along it. Then he covered the tape with fabric. The fabric kept the tape from losing its stickiness until it was ready for use. Earle hung a strip of his ready-made bandages in the kitchen.

Josephine loved her husband's new invention. She still cut and burned herself all the time. But now, when she did, she could treat her own wound. She could slice off a length of bandage. Then she could peel off the fabric. She could apply the bandage without help. Earle's co-workers liked his invention too. They told Dickson to share his idea with the boss. He did.

Earle's boss liked his idea. But it was not an instant success. The bandage strip was given no brand name. It was too large to be useful. Johnson and Johnson worked to improve the product. They gave it a name. Now Earle's idea became a big hit. He was made vice president of Johnson and Johnson. A machine was created to make bandages in many sizes. Mrs. Dickson's kitchen troubles brought us Band-Aids®.

 0-7696-3395-1 *Inventions*

Comprehension

Circle the best answer. Highlight the sentence or sentences in the story where you find the answer.

1. Soap . . .

    a. was invented in 1878.

    b. has been around for thousands of years.

    c. was first used to wash dishes.

    d. was used more five thousand years ago than it is today.

2. Ivory® Soap . . .

    a. floated the first time it was made.

    b. was almost called P&G soap.

    c. was once gray in color.

    d. was invented by a kid.

3. The first batch of Ivory® Soap to float did so because . . .

    a. it is lighter than other soaps.

    b. it is white.

    c. it was cooked too long.

    d. it was made of pumice stone.

4. Ivory® Soap floats today . . .

    a. because soap makers don't know how to make it sink.

    b. only when a batch is cooked too long.

    c. because air is whipped into it.

    d. because air is removed from it.

5. Adhesive bandages . . .

    a. replaced gauze bandages and medical tape.

    b. were invented by Josephine Dickson.

    c. were invented in a factory.

    d. are difficult to put on.

Clean It Off and Bandage It: The Inventions of Ivory Soap® and Band-Aids®

6. Josephine Dickson . . .
   a. worked for Johnson and Johnson.
   b. was accident-prone.
   c. was a great cook.
   d. was an old woman when her husband invented Band-Aids®.

7. Which was the order of applying a bandage before the invention of adhesive tapes?
   a. cut gauze–tape gauze in place–fold gauze–cut tape
   b. tape gauze in place–cut tape–fold gauze–cut gauze
   c. cut gauze–fold gauze–cut tape–tape gauze in place
   d. cut tape–fold gauze–cut gauze–tape gauze in place

8. Josephine's husband . . .
   a. did all the cooking.
   b. quit his job to take care of her frequent injuries.
   c. was a teacher.
   d. placed folded pieces of gauze on a long strip of tape.

9. Earle covered his gauze and tape with fabric . . .
   a. to make his wife's bandages more attractive.
   b. so the tape wouldn't lose its stickiness before use.
   c. to make his wife's bandages softer.
   d. so bandage strips would sell better.

10. Adhesive bandages did not sell well at first because . . .
    a. they were too large and had no name brand.
    b. consumers did not trust they would work.
    c. it was just as easy to cover wounds with gauze and medical tape.
    d. they were intended for use with animals, not people.

Discussion Questions

1. Why might floating white soap sell better than sinking gray soap?

2. It's difficult to imagine life without adhesive bandages. What other inventions do we take for granted today? How would life be different without each of the inventions you discussed?

3. Soap was once thought useful only for cleaning wounds. Frequent use was said to dry your skin out too much. What medical or hygiene advice has changed during your lifetime?

Create a Timeline

Look back at the story to help you fill in the timeline below with events in the history of soap.

3000 B.C._____

A.D. 100_____

1878 _____

1879 _____

1891 _____

Clean It Off and Bandage It: The Inventions of Ivory Soap® and Band-Aids®

Vocabulary Activities

Circle the word that doesn't belong in each set of words.

1. adhesive   tape   glue   paint

2. remember   oversight   forget   ignore

3. detergent   wallpaper   soap   cleanser

4. trendy   fashionable   vogue   unpopular

5. froth   foam   chocolate   bubbly

6. injury   gauze   bandage   Band-Aid®

7. diligent   lazy   determined   doggedly

Homework

Write an imaginary story using all the words you circled above.

Extension

What brand of soap do you use? How about your friends? Conduct a soap survey of your classmates. Graph your results.

Clean It Off and Bandage It: The Inventions of Ivory Soap® and Band-Aids®

Name _____ Date _____

Prereading Activities

Looking It Over

1. Read the title of the article that begins on page 26.

2. Leaf through the pages of the article, stopping to look at the pictures.

3. Read the list of vocabulary words.

What Do You Know?

List all of the uses you can think of for Velcro® fasteners.

_____

_____

About how many teddy bears can be found in your house?

_____

_____

Make a Prediction

How can nature inspire inventions?

_____

_____

_____

What do you think this reading will be about?

_____

_____

_____

Read the article to add to your knowledge.

Vocabulary

gesture   something said or done to express an emotion

Example: Sending your aunt a birthday card was a kind gesture.

engaged   hooked, attached

Example: The buckle engaged the hole in the strap, and the belt was fastened.

prism   a shape that separates light into colors

Example: A prism displays a rainbow of colors.

periscope   an instrument used for seeing at an angle

Example: Periscopes allow sailors on submarines to see above water.

prototype   a first, sample version

Example: Before de Mestral could sell his idea, he had to make a prototype.

venture   a risky business move

Example: Ulyana's used book selling ventures paid off when she opened her own store.

25   0-7696-3395-1 *Inventions*

Nature Inspires: Teddy Bears and Velcro® Fasteners

Countless inventors must thank Mother Nature for great ideas. Looking at prisms in nature led to the periscope. Lightning inspired Ben Franklin's work. Gravity was first observed in a bathtub. Georges de Mestral credits burs for his invention. The Teddy bear is so-called thanks to a hunting trip.

de Mestral's Fasteners

One spring day in the 1940s, Georges de Mestral went for a walk. He took his dog along. The two were covered in burs when they got home. de Mestral picked the burs from his pants. He picked them from his socks and coat. He picked them from his dog's fur. As he did, he thought of a question. What made burs stick so well? de Mestral looked at a corner of his coat under a microscope. He saw that hooks on burs engaged in loops on fabric. This gave de Mestral an idea.

0-7696-3395-1 *Inventions*

de Mestral was sure a fastener could work in the same way a bur does. Strips of hooks could be attached to strips of loops. The results could keep pants closed and pockets from emptying. He was sure of it, but no one else was. Finally, he talked with a weaver in France. The man agreed to help de Mestral make a prototype.

Producing the first strip of fastening tape was easy. The two men just worked until the strip looked like the image in de Mestral's head. Mass producing the product was not so easy. There were no machines designed to make the tape. de Mestral experimented. He learned that nylon sewn under infrared light created loops.

de Mestral was on his way. He opened factories. He began selling his product worldwide. In 20 years he was making 60 million yards of it a year. Today Velcro® offers hundreds of products. It attaches mini clocks to car dashes. It closes tent flaps. It keeps shoes tight and pockets secure. It even secures equipment on space shuttles. de Mestral turned a lesson from Mother Nature into a multimillion-dollar venture.

0-7696-3395-1 *Inventions*

Teddy's Bear

Nature Inspires: Teddy Bears and Velcro® Fasteners

One day in 1902, President Teddy Roosevelt was in Mississippi. He had just settled a border dispute. Now he wanted to hunt. Roosevelt liked many outdoor ventures. He often went on hikes. He also liked to swim and jog. On this trip, he wanted to hunt.

Roosevelt was a renowned hunter. Many of the big game he shot now line a wall at the Smithsonian. On this day in 1902, Roosevelt was not doing well. In fact, it looked like he would not take home a single skin. One of the men with him tied a small bear cub to a tree. He thought Roosevelt would kill the cub. The President did not see the sport in hunting a young, captured animal. He refused to shoot.

Clifford Berryman was with the President that day. He was a political cartoonist. Berryman was impressed with Roosevelt's gesture. He drew a cartoon about the hunt. It showed the President refusing to shoot the bear cub. The line under the picture was a play on words. It talked about the border dispute and the hunt. It read: "Drawing the line in Mississippi." The cartoon ran in many papers. After that, all Berryman cartoons about Roosevelt showed the bear in one corner. It became known as "Teddy's bear."

A store owner in New York liked "Teddy's bear." Morris Mitchom asked his wife to sew a stuffed bear like the cartoon one. Mitchom placed the bear in his store window. Beside it was a copy of Berryman's cartoon. In no time, Mitchom was bombarded with orders for "Teddy bears."

At the same time, Richard Steiff was selling stuffed fabric bears in Germany. At a toy show, a New York man saw Steiff's bears. He ordered 3,000 units.

Then luck struck. In 1906, Teddy Roosevelt's daughter got married. Someone in charge of decorating saw one of Steiff's bears in New York. He purchased several. He dressed each bear in outdoor wear. There were fishermen bears. There were hunter bears. There were hiking bears. One bear was placed at each table at the wedding reception. One of the guests asked the President what breed the bears represented. He did not know. A guest answered for the President. He said, "They're Teddy's bears, of course."

0-7696-3395-1 *Inventions*

Comprehension

Circle the best answer. Highlight the sentence or sentences in the story where you find each answer.

1. The Teddy bear was named after . . .
   a. Theodore Geisel, who is known as Dr. Seuss.
   b. President Franklin Roosevelt.
   c. President Teddy Roosevelt.
   d. its inventor, Ted Stone.

2. Some of the outdoor activities Teddy Roosevelt liked were . . .
   a. swimming, hiking, jogging, and hunting.
   b. swimming and tennis.
   c. hiking and golf.
   d. jogging, swimming, and archery.

3. When Roosevelt neglected to kill anything during a hunt . . .
   a. he became angry.
   b. one of his companions killed a bear for him.
   c. someone tied a bear cub to a tree for him to shoot.
   d. he shot a bear cub someone captured for him.

4. Roosevelt's daughter's wedding reception was decorated with . . .
   a. flowers.
   b. Roosevelt-look-alike dolls.
   c. stuffed bears dressed in wedding gowns.
   d. stuffed bears dressed in outdoor wear.

5. Who drew a cartoon about Roosevelt's hunting trip?
   a. Richard Steiff
   b. Morris Mitchom
   c. Clifford Berryman
   d. Samuel Smithsonian

6. Teddy Bears and Velcro® fasteners have what in common?
   a. They were both inspired by something that happened in nature.
   b. They use the same kind of fabric.
   c. They were invented in the same year.
   d. They were invented by the same man.

7. What plant inspired de Mestral?
   a. thistles
   b. burs
   c. daisies
   d. poison ivy

8. de Mestral thought Velcro® would be useful for . . .
   a. keeping pants and pockets closed.
   b. closing purses.
   c. hanging posters to walls.
   d. taking burs out of socks and sweaters.

9. de Mestral created the loops for his fasteners . . .
   a. by himself.
   b. by sewing nylon under infrared light.
   c. out of plastic.
   d. using real burs.

10. Velcro® products . . .
    a. are limited to about 10 varieties.
    b. are sold only in North America.
    c. secure equipment aboard space shuttles.
    d. never made much money for de Mestral.

Discussion Questions

1. How did nature inspire the two inventions in this article?

2. Why do you think stuffed bears are more popular than other stuffed animals?

3. Have you ever noticed something in nature that gave you the idea for a great invention? Talk about it.

Prove It!

Find and copy three supporting sentences from the reading that prove each of these points.

1. Georges de Mestral was a curious man.

_____

_____

_____

2. President Teddy Roosevelt was an outdoorsman.

_____

_____

_____

3. Velcro® works like burs attaching to fabric.

_____

_____

_____

Vocabulary Activities

Write sentences that include each pair of words.

1. prism, periscope

_____

_____

_____

2. venture, engaged

_____

_____

_____

3. prototype, gesture

_____

_____

_____

Homework

Write an imaginative story about how your favorite game or toy got its name.

Extension

Research and report on the history of fasteners in fashion from buttons to belts to zippers.

Nature Inspires: Teddy Bears and Velcro® Fasteners

Name _____   Date _____

 # Prereading Activities

Looking It Over

1. Read the title of the article that begins on page 36.

2. Leaf through the pages of the article, stopping to look at the pictures.

3. Read the list of vocabulary words.

What Do You Know?

List any inventions you know to be connected to times of war.

_____

_____

_____

Make a Prediction

Silly Putty® and the Slinky® were both intended to be used for other purposes. What might scientists have intended the uses of each to be?

_____

_____

_____

_____

_____

Read the article to add to your knowledge.

Vocabulary

patent   a paper giving legal ownership to an idea

Example: Applying for a patent will assure you get credit for your new invention.

advances   improvements

Example: Advances in aviation have resulted in quicker planes.

icon   a culturally popular symbol

Example: The Slinky® has become an American icon.

gear   equipment

Example: When you go camping, don't forget your hiking gear.

continent   a division of land on the globe

Example: Deer are native to the North American continent.

engineers   people trained to create things

Example: Engineers worked on improving airplanes during World War II.

By-Products of War: Silly Putty® and the Slinky®

On December 7, 1941, the United States entered World War II. Thousands of soldiers were called to service in Europe. Countless others helped the war effort from home. Women knitted gloves and hats. Bankers sold war bonds. Inventors used their creativity to meet the demands of the war. Improvements were made on airplanes. Breakthroughs were made in plastics. Advances were made in medicine.

Not every battle soldiers fought overseas was won. Not every effort made at home was successful either. Still, we won the war. And we got some pretty cool toys out of the deal. Two wartime failures turned out to be successes after all.

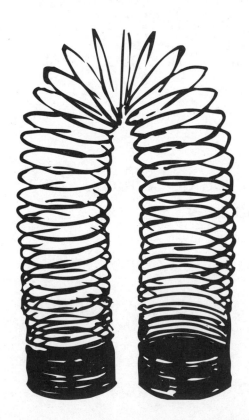

The Slinky®

Richard James worked on the World War II war effort from home. He tried to make a spring that could hold gear still on a moving warship. Each time a spring didn't work, he stacked it on a shelf above his desk. One day, James bumped one of the failed springs. The falling metal coil took a strange path. It spilled from the shelf to a book on James's desk. Then it tumbled to the desktop. Then it flopped to the floor. There it rested upright. James tried to repeat the journey. Sure enough, the spring flopped along its path again. It made the same motion when climbing down stairs.

0-7696-3395-1 *Inventions*

James shared his find with his wife and kids. Soon every kid in town knew about the walking spring. James thought the simple, unpainted metal spring could be a toy. James's wife searched the dictionary for a name for the item. James found a machine shop that would coil and cut wire. By Christmas of 1945, the world's first Slinky® was ready for sale. The product was showed to shoppers at a store in Philadelphia. Four hundred springs were sold in less than 90 minutes.

The Jameses borrowed $500. They built a machine that could turn 80 feet of wire into a spring in 10 seconds. By the next year, the war that started James working with springs was over. But the Slinky® had just begun its success.

The Slinky® lives on. The machines James invented 50 years ago have changed very little. The classic Slinky® looks pretty much the same, too. Over 50 types of the toy sell today. But the basic walking spring still amuses the most. The classic Slinky® sells more units than any other variety.

More than 250 million Slinkys® have sold to date. The toy has appeared in movies. It can be seen on a postage stamp. You can buy one made of gold. You can pick up one on every continent of the world except Antarctica. The Jameses turned a rejected warship spring into an American icon.

Silly Putty®

Silly Putty® was first made during World War II as well. Some men tried to make a substitute for rubber in those years. None was successful. Still, more than one of them claims to have made Silly Putty® instead.

Rob Roy McGregor and Earl Warrick worked for Corning Glass Works at the time. They applied for a patent for a putty mixture in 1943. James Wright of General Electric tried for a similar patent. Neither recipe was a good double for rubber. In fact, none of the men could think of a use for the pink stuff they made. Peter Hodgson could.

0-7696-3395-1 *Inventions*

Wright won the patent war for Silly Putty®. But he did not name the stuff. And he did not make money off the product. Hodgson did those things. Wright shared his putty with engineers around the globe. He hoped one of them could come up with a use for the stuff. None of them did. But one of them showed the "gupp" to some friends. One of his friends was Hodgson. Hodgson thought the pink stuff would make a good toy. He convinced a friend to try to sell the stuff through her toy catalog. The putty was placed in clear cases. Each case sold for $2.00.

Hodgson borrowed $147. He bought the rights to the strange putty and 21 pounds of the stuff. He called the "gupp" Silly Putty®. He divided his putty into small balls. Since Easter was near, he placed each ball in a plastic egg. It was not an instant success. But it has shown staying power.

By the time of his death, Hodgson was worth $140 million. Nearly two million eggs of Silly Putty® are sold each year in the United States alone. The stuff comes in classic, glow-in-the-dark, glitter, and fluorescent colors now. Silly Putty® never replaced rubber. But it is still popular 50 years after its invention.

Comprehension

Circle the best answer. Highlight the sentence or sentences in the story where you find each answer.

1. How did people at home help with the World War II effort?
   a. Women knitted gloves and hats.
   b. Bankers sold war bonds.
   c. Scientists tried to create substitutes for expensive materials.
   d. All of the above.

2. The Slinky® and Silly Putty® . . .
   a. were both wartime failures turned toy success.
   b. were both useful to soldiers during World War II.
   c. were both created during World War I.
   d. were both invented by the same man.

3. The Slinky® was first sold . . .
   a. around Easter in Philadelphia.
   b. around Christmas in Chicago.
   c. around Christmas in Philadelphia.
   d. around Easter in Chicago.

4. Who invented the Slinky®?
   a. Richard James
   b. Rob Roy McGregor
   c. Earl Warrick
   d. Peter Hodgson

5. The Slinky® . . .
   a. comes in glow-in-the-dark colors.
   b. rights were bought for $147.00.
   c. has sold 250 million units.
   d. first sold for $2.00 each.

6. Silly Putty® . . .
  a. has been pictured on a postage stamp.
  b. is sold in 50 different varieties.
  c. was first manufactured by a $500 machine.
  d. comes in fluorescent colors.

7. Who won the patent war for Silly Putty®?
  a. James Richards
  b. James Wright
  c. Peter Hodgson
  d. Rob McGregor

8. Silly Putty® was first sold . . .
  a. around Christmas.
  b. in a grocery store.
  c. by its inventor.
  d. through a toy catalog.

9. By the time of his death, Hodgson was worth . . .
  a. $140 million.
  b. nearly $1 million.
  c. $250 million.
  d. little more than he was before Silly Putty®'s invention.

10. During World War II, no improvements were made in . . .
  a. plastics.
  b. medicine.
  c. aviation.
  d. rubber.

By-Products of War: Silly Putty® and the Slinky®

Discussion Questions

1. If we never went to war again, would we notice a slowdown in technological advancements? Why, or why not?

2. James Wright asked everyone he knew if they could think of a use for Silly Putty®. What have you used it for? What else could it be used for?

3. Talk about the many ways in which you have used a spring.

Silly Stuff

Compare and contrast the Slinky® and Silly Putty® with this Venn diagram.

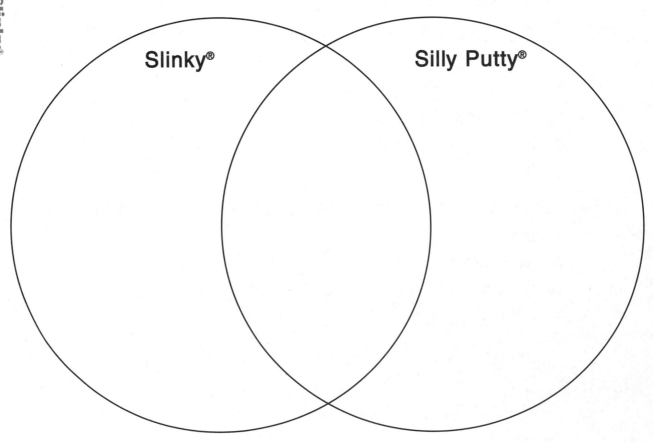

Vocabulary Activities

Antonyms are opposites. Synonyms are similar. Decide whether each pair of words are antonyms or synonyms. Circle your responses.

1. advance: destroy   antonyms   synonyms

2. icon: symbol   antonyms   synonyms

3. gear: equipment   antonyms   synonyms

4. patented copy: pirated copy   antonyms   synonyms

5. engineer: scientist   antonyms   synonyms

Homework

Draw a picture and write a description of an invention you would like to get patented.

Extension

Research and report on other World War II inventions.

By-Products of War: Silly Putty® and the Slinky®

Prereading Activities

Looking It Over

1. Read the title of the article that begins on page 46.

2. Leaf through the pages of the article, stopping to look at the pictures.

3. Read the list of vocabulary words.

What Do You Know?

List different kinds of doughnuts.

_____

_____

In what ways is rubber used today?

_____

_____

Make a Prediction

Rubber and doughnuts are much more popular today than they used to be. What improvements might have been made to rubber to make it useful? How might doughnuts of old have been different than they are today?

_____

_____

_____

_____

Read the article to add to your knowledge.

 0-7696-3395-1 *Inventions*

Vocabulary

valve
something that controls the flow of liquid or air

Example: A valve in your life jacket allows you to add or release air.

brittle
easily broken or snapped

Example: Bones become brittle if you do not get enough calcium.

dedicate
set aside for a special purpose

Example: Charles Goodyear dedicated his life to improving rubber.

enlisted
got the help of

Example: Hanson Crockett Gregory enlisted the help of his mom in making doughnuts.

absorb
soak up

Example: Sponges can absorb a lot of liquid.

indebted
to owe

Example: Automobile drivers are indebted to Goodyear for the improvements he made in rubber.

institution
establishment

Example: Doughnuts have become an American institution.

Making Great Strides: Improvements in Doughnuts and Rubber

Doughnuts and rubber have been around for a long time. But neither was very popular until a few changes were made.

Remaking Rubber

Charles Goodyear had a hard life. He did not finish high school. So he worked for his dad. Then his dad's store closed. Goodyear decided to make things. He invented a valve for life jackets. He tried to sell his idea. But the rubber company in his town could not buy it. They had very little money. Few people were buying rubber. That's because it melted in the heat. It got brittle in the cold.

Goodyear knew rubber could be useful. It was elastic. It was waterproof. If only it could handle temperature changes. Goodyear decided to dedicate the rest of his life to making rubber work. But first he had to serve time in prison. Goodyear had not sold his valve idea. He had no other job. He had a wife and children to care for. Goodyear had bills he could not pay. In the 1800s, that meant he had to go to prison.

0-7696-3395-1 *Inventions*

As soon as Goodyear served his time, he returned to his work with rubber. He borrowed money from friends. He rented a laboratory. He enlisted his wife's help in mixing countless batches of smelly gum rubber. They added different powders to the gooey rubber. Goodyear hoped one of them would absorb rubber's stickiness. Some of the powders worked a little bit. But none was just right. Then an accident happened.

Goodyear was proud of his latest batch of rubber. Adding sulfur seemed to make it less sticky. He grabbed a handful of the stuff and ran to a store where his friends were talking. He waved the rubber in the air, bragging to his friends. A piece of rubber flew out of Goodyear's hand. It landed on the hot potbellied stove in the middle of the room. When heated, the sulfur-treated rubber was perfect. It was strong. It was elastic. It did not melt in the heat. It did not get brittle in the cold. It was very useful. In fact, rubber found so many uses it made many people millionaires. Unfortunately, Charles Goodyear was not one of them.

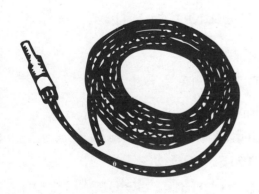

Goodyear did not apply for patents. He sold his sulfur recipe to a rubber plant. He did not care about money. He cared about rubber. He worked with rubber his whole life. He made his calling card out of rubber. He wore a rubber tie. He ate off rubber plates. He had a self-portrait done in rubber. He wrote his autobiography in rubber. When he died, Goodyear was $200,000 in debt. But today, we are all indebted to the man who made rubber work!

Who Put the Hole in the Doughnut?

The story of the doughnut hole is something of a mystery. Hanson Crockett Gregory did not write down what happened. He did not patent his invention. So the story of doughnut holes has a few holes of its own.

This much is true. Dutch-Germans moved to Pennsylvania in the 1700s. They brought with them a recipe for oil cakes. Oil cakes were circles of dough. They had apples, raisins, or nuts in their centers. The cakes were deep-fried. Then they were dipped in sugar. Before long, people all over America were eating oil cakes.

0-7696-3395-1 *Inventions*

Here's where the questions begin. Doughnuts are oil cakes. But how and why did they get holes in the middle? Some historians credit Hanson Crockett Gregory. Gregory was a sea captain. When he visited home between voyages, his mother wanted to cook foods Gregory loved. Gregory loved doughnuts. But sometimes the middle of doughnuts didn't fry well. They stayed doughy. Gregory didn't like that. One day, he is said to have poked holes in doughnut dough. His mother fried the doughnuts with the holes in the middle. The holes allowed the hot oil to cook the entire doughnut. The practice caught on.

Maybe Gregory was the first to put the hole in doughnuts. A plaque in Rockport, Maine, says he was. Still, the young man did not patent his idea. John F. Blondel did. Twenty-five years after Gregory poked his holes in doughnuts, Blondel claimed the idea in 1872.

Today, doughnuts come with and without holes. They come with fillings and toppings. They can be bought in grocery stores. They can be found in cafes and doughnut shops. We eat doughnuts for breakfast. We eat them at social gatherings. We eat them at parties. Thanks to Gregory and Blondel, they have become an American institution.

Comprehension

Circle the best answer. Highlight the sentence or sentences in the story where you find each answer.

1. Charles Goodyear had a hard start at adult life because . . .
   a. he did not finish high school.
   b. his dad's store closed down.
   c. the rubber company in his town did not buy his idea.
   d. all of the above.

2. The major problem with early rubber was . . .
   a. it could not handle temperature changes.
   b. it was not waterproof.
   c. is was not very elastic.
   d. it was neon pink in color.

3. Goodyear had to go to prison because . . .
   a. he didn't pay his taxes.
   b. he neglected his children.
   c. he couldn't pay his bills.
   d. he stole rubber products from factories.

4. Goodyear's best batch of rubber is called an accident because . . .
   a. he didn't mean to spill sulfur in it.
   b. he cooked it too long.
   c. he didn't cook it long enough.
   d. it was heated by accident when Goodyear dropped a piece on a potbellied stove.

5. Goodyear did not make which of these items out of rubber?
   a. his bed
   b. a self-portrait
   c. a tie
   d. plates

6. Goodyear's improvements on rubber . . .
   a. made him a rich man.
   b. did not help rubber sell any better.
   c. took him less than six weeks to perfect.
   d. never made him a rich man.

7. We cannot be certain of Gregory's role in the history of doughnut holes because . . .
   a. his patent did not include many details.
   b. he did not write his story down.
   c. Gregory was a known liar.
   d. Gregory never liked doughnuts.

8. Oil cakes were like doughnuts except . . .
   a. they each had four holes in them.
   b. they were filled with chocolate chips.
   c. they were not fried.
   d. they did not have holes.

9. Gregory is said to have poked a hole in a doughnut because he wanted . . .
   a. to play a trick on his brother.
   b. the doughnut to cook all the way through.
   c. to try baking the dough instead of frying it.
   d. to eat the resulting round "doughnut hole."

10. Which is a true statement about doughnuts?
   a. Gregory patented his doughnut hole idea.
   b. Doughnuts came from France.
   c. John F. Blondel patented the doughnut hole.
   d. Before they had holes, doughnuts were called crumb cakes.

Discussion Questions

1. What improvements made rubber and the doughnut popular? Do you think either of them would be around today without the improvements?

2. Goodyear dedicated his life to his work. What are the pros and cons of a person dedicating his life to his work?

3. The story of the doughnut hole is kind of an urban legend. Tell about other stories you know of that contain questionable facts.

The Doughnut Game

Complete the following questions as fast as you can. Which student in your class finished first?

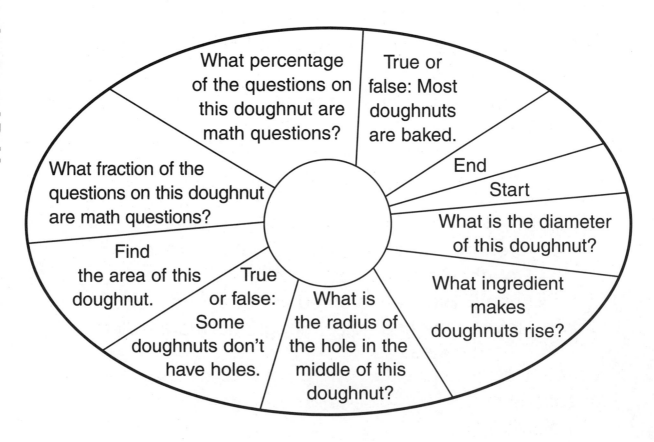

Vocabulary Activities

Which word from the Word Bank is related to each of the sentences below? Write your answers in the spaces provided.

> **Word Bank**
>
> | valve | brittle | dedicate | enlist |
> |-------|---------|----------|--------|
> | absorb | indebted | institution | |

_____ 1. The ceremony at the new park celebrated the special place for the town's kids to play.

_____ 2. Some plastics crack and break when frozen.

_____ 3. A sponge can soak up a lot of liquid.

_____ 4. I need to get lots of people to help me move.

_____ 5. You need a way to blow up that beach ball.

_____ 6. We owe gratitude to Goodyear for his work with rubber.

_____ 7. School is a learning establishment.

Homework

Write ten trivia questions about the history of rubber or doughnut holes based on the reading. Quiz your friends.

Extension

Create a board game, playing pieces, rules, and more questions to develop your homework assignment into a complete game.

Prereading Activities

Looking It Over

1. Read the title of the article that begins on page 56.

2. Leaf through the pages of the article, stopping to look at the pictures.

3. Read the list of vocabulary words.

What Do You Know?

List items that make use of a zipper.

_____

_____

_____

List foods that include chocolate chips.

_____

_____

_____

Make a Prediction

What do you think this article will be about? What could zippers and chocolate chips have in common?

_____

_____

_____

_____

Read the article to add to your knowledge.

Vocabulary

device a specialized tool

Example: Nestle® candy bars used to be sold with a device for chopping them.

industry manufacturing operations

Example: Chocolate products are a large industry.

sport (verb) show or display

Example: At the office, I sport a tie.

remodeled made improvements on a structure

Example: Mr. Wakefield remodeled the Toll House Inn.

region area

Example: The Toll House Inn became the favorite restaurant in New England.

locals people who live in an area

Example: Visitors liked to stay at the Toll House Inn, but locals loved to eat their desserts.

Zip and Chip: Step-by-Step Inventions

Both the zipper and the chocolate chip were a long time in the making!

Zip It Up

Clothes fasteners have been used for centuries. Leather belts used to be worn around loose styles. Bone pins clipped clothes at the shoulder. Laces and hooks kept boots on feet. Then buttons were invented. They were made of wood, glass, horn, bone, brass, and gems. Not until the twentieth century did a new fastener take hold of the market. It was imagined before that. But it took 80 years to perfect the zipper.

It all started in 1851. Elias Howe was an idea man. He made one of the first sewing machines. He also patented a zipper-like device. But he never tried to sell his idea. Forty-four years later, Whitcomb Judson did.

Judson was an idea man, too. In the 1800s, people used hooks and laces on boots. Judson thought this was a lot of work. He made a "clasp-locker." It was meant to replace hooks and laces. It was a lot like Howe's device. Judson tried to sell his idea at a World's Fair. He rented a booth. He showed people how to use his product. People watched, but most of them didn't buy. In fact, Judson made only one sale. The U.S. Postal Service bought 20 clasp-lockers. They used them on mailbags.

Judson started a company to make more clasp-lockers. He thought his product would catch on. It didn't. Then Judson's daughter got married. Her husband was Gideon Sundback. He was an engineer. When Judson and his daughter died, Sundback was sad. He poured himself into his work. His work was improving the clasp-locker.

0-7696-3395-1 *Inventions*

In 1917, Sundback patented the "separable fastener." It looked like a modern zipper. It was first used by the army. It closed soldiers' bags during battle. Next it appeared on Goodrich rubber boots. B. F. Goodrich coined the term *zipper.* He thought the fasteners made a zipping sound.

Goodrich's boots made the zipper a great success. Still, it was limited in use. For 30 years, zippers appeared only on boots and tobacco pouches. Finally the fashion industry brought the zipper into the public eye. Ads said zippers could help kids dress themselves. They showed how zippers would work well on men's pants. Today, zippers are found on countless products. Everything from clothes to luggage, tents, and purses sport zippers today.

First the Chocolate, Then the Chip

In 1930, new owners bought the Toll House Inn. The Wakefields knew the lodge had a rich history. Stagecoaches once stopped there. Drivers paid a toll. Horses rested. Travelers ate a hot meal at the stop. Sometimes they stayed all night. Now Ken and Ruth Wakefield wanted to make the Massachusetts inn a famous stop again.

Ken remodeled the inn. Ruth prepared a New England menu. The couple did a fine job. The Toll House Inn gained a new life. It became a favorite stop for visitors to the region. Ruth's desserts became popular with the locals.

0-7696-3395-1 *Inventions*

One day Ruth decided to offer a new dessert. She cut a few chunks off a chocolate bar. She added the chunks to a batch of butter cookies. Ruth thought adding chocolate to them would create rich, brown cookies. Ruth was wrong. Her cookies stayed white. They were only spotted with melted chocolate. Ruth served her surprising outcome. Her guests were pleased.

The new cookie became a Toll House Inn favorite. A Boston newspaper ran Ruth's recipe. Smaller newspapers did, too. Toll House guests spread the word to friends. New England was buying Nestle® semi-sweet candy bars in record numbers.

Those same candy bars were not selling well in other parts of the nation. In fact, the company was going to stop making them. First they sent a salesman to New England. He was to find out why sales were so good there. Locals told him about Ruth's cookies. They took him to the Toll House Inn. The company decided not to stop making their semi-sweet bar. Instead, they printed Ruth's recipe on their candy wrappers.

The nation liked Ruth's cookies. The company began to make lines on their candy bars so they could be broken easier. Next, it packaged a chopping device with the bar. Finally, it began to chunk the bars before sales. In 1939, the chocolate chip cookie gave birth to the chocolate chip.

Comprehension

Circle the best answer. Highlight the sentence or sentences in the story where you find your answer.

1. The zipper was envisioned how many years before it became popular?
   a. 10
   b. 30
   c. 50
   d. 80

2. Elias Howe not only imagined the zipper but also invented . . .
   a. the refrigerator.
   b. the iron.
   c. the sewing machine.
   d. the microwave.

3. What did Elias Howe do with his zipper idea?
   a. He tried to sell it.
   b. He used it on his own clothes.
   c. He kept it a secret.
   d. He patented it.

4. Whitcomb Judson thought "clasp-lockers" would work well on . . .
   a. suitcases.
   b. boots.
   c. dresses.
   d. jeans.

5. The only buyer of "clasp-lockers" was . . .
   a. a grocery store chain.
   b. a clothing store owner.
   c. the United States Army.
   d. the United States Postal Service.

6. Sundback's "separable fastener" first appeared on . . .

    a. raincoats.

    b. rubber boots.

    c. winter jackets.

    d. pants.

7. Toll House Cookies were named after . . .

    a. the inn owned by their creator.

    b. a tollbooth in Indiana.

    c. the factory that makes them.

    d. a town in Massachusetts.

8. Chocolate chips . . .

    a. were created after chocolate chip cookies.

    b. were first used for making chocolate cake.

    c. were invented by Ruth Wakefield.

    d. were used in the first chocolate chip cookie recipes.

9. Nestle® was going to stop making their semi-sweet candy bars because . . .

    a. they were hard to manufacture.

    b. they were not selling well in much of the country.

    c. they did not taste good.

    d. they wanted to replace it with something better.

10. Ruth and Ken Wakefield owned . . .

    a. a newspaper.

    b. a bakery.

    c. an inn and restaurant.

    d. a grocery store.

Discussion Questions

1. What is ironic about the invention of the chocolate chip?

2. Advertising helped make zippers popular with the public. Talk about items that are popular today mostly due to their advertising. What kind of products sell well without heavy advertising?

3. Ruth Wakefield expected her cookies to come out of the oven brown. She served her "mistake" at her restaurant anyway. Talk about a "mistake" you have made that turned out pretty good.

Identifying Fasteners

What type of fasteners are being described here? Record your responses in the spaces provided.

_____ 1. long, thin fasteners found on shoes

_____ 2. metal dots that make a sound when fastened together

_____ 3. held in place with pant loops

_____ 4. plastic circles that fit through slits

_____ 5. metal or plastic teeth that interlock

_____ 6. fabric strips that stick together

Vocabulary Activities

Fill in the blanks in these sentences with words from the Word Bank.

> **Word Bank**
>
> | device | industry | sport |
> | remodeled | region | locals |

1. The _____ of the region especially liked Ruth's desserts.

2. A chopping _____ was once sold with candy bars.

3. The music _____ sells CDs and concert tickets.

4. Chocolate chip bags sometimes _____ cookie recipes.

5. The Midwest _____ of the United States includes Michigan and Illinois.

6. Ken Wakefield _____ the Toll House Inn.

Homework

Write a recipe to be included in a classroom book of favorite foods.

Extension

Try cooking the recipes from your new classroom recipe book.

Prereading Activities

Looking It Over

1. Read the title of the article that begins on page 66.

2. Leaf through the pages of the article, stopping to look at the pictures.

3. Read the list of vocabulary words.

What Do You Know?

List all the kinds of chewing gum you have tried.

_____

_____

How is ice cream made? What are your favorite kinds of ice cream?

_____

_____

Make a Prediction

What might this article be about? What is an "invention by chance"?

_____

_____

_____

_____

_____

Read the article to add to your knowledge.

Vocabulary

resin   tree sap

              Example: Ancient people chewed resin instead of gum.

ancient   from the faraway past

              Example: There was no written language in ancient times.

plant   factory

              Example: Gum is now manufactured in a gum-making plant.

tropical   relating to the region around the equator

              Example: I like tropical fruit-flavored ice cream.

carnivals   fairs or festivals

              Example: I ride the roller coaster that comes to town with the carnival each year.

vendor   a person who sells something

              Example: A waffle vendor and an ice cream vendor got together to create the waffle cone.

scarce   not readily available

              Example: Tree sap became scarce when it was used as a chewing gum base.

Inventions by Chance: Chewing Gum and Ice Cream

Some of the most fun things we chew on have the most interesting history.

Chewing Gum Hits the Big Time

Chewing gum was more of a discovery than an invention. Ancient people chewed grass, wax, leaves, and tree resin. These things freshened their breath. They exercised people's jaws. Europeans who came to America found natives chewing on spruce tree resin. But it would be another hundred years before gum was sold at stores.

John Curtis opened the first gum-making plant in the world. He was a logger who lived in Maine. In 1848, he stopped cutting down spruce trees. He began collecting their resin instead. He used the tree resin to make gum. Within two years, 200 people worked for Curtis. But spruce tree resin became scarce. It was hard to turn into gum, too. So people tried to make gum from wax. It was too stiff.

0-7696-3395-1 *Inventions*

Then a new gum base was tried. It did not come from the United States. It came from the Yucatan Peninsula. It made its way to our country because of a war. Mexico lost the Mexican-American War of 1846–1847. At the end of the war, General Santa Anna was kicked out of his country. He moved to New York. He brought chicle with him. Chicle is milky and waxy. It comes from trees in tropical forests.

Thomas Adams was the first man to make gum of chicle. But that is not what he set out to do. He saw Santa Anna chewing chicle in New York one day. Thomas Adams thought the chewy stuff would make a good substitute for rubber. He experimented with the tree sap. He tried many things, but he could not make chicle act like rubber. So he added flavorings to chicle instead. He started selling gum.

Black Jack gum was Adams's first brand. Within 20 years, other people were making gum, too. Still, some people did not like gum. Dentists said chewing gum would hurt your jaws. Doctors said gum would stick to your intestines. Rumors said that gum was made of glue and horse hooves. Some people said chewing it was impolite, or even evil.

67

Gum companies fought hard to win customers. They added trading cards to their packages. They gave bonus gifts to people who bought gum. William Wrigley Jr. even sent a stick of gum to everyone in the U.S. phone book! Their ideas worked. Chewing gum was here to stay. Today, Americans chew $2.5 billion worth of gum each year. That is an average of 300 sticks per person!

Ice Cream

In the late 1800s, sodas were sold in soda shops and at carnivals. Flavorings were mixed into soda water to make the drinks. One day, a man selling sodas at a fair ran out of flavorings. So he bought ice cream from another vendor. He put the ice cream in his sodas. The ice cream soda was born.

By 1904, people were making their own sodas. They just mixed a soda powder into water. One day an 11-year-old boy made a soda. He put it on the porch to chill. Then he forgot about it. It stayed on the porch overnight. When the boy woke, his soda was frozen. The popsicle was born.

Some people thought sodas were sinfully delicious. A town in Illinois outlawed their sale on Sundays. Soda shop owners found a way around the law. They served ice cream sodas without the soda. Syrup-covered ice cream was great. Ice cream sundaes were born.

The waffle cone was born at a huge fair in Louisiana. Ernest A. Hamwi was selling crisp waffles there. A young man beside him was selling ice cream in a bowl. The young man ran out of bowls. He bought waffles from Hamwi. He rolled the waffles into cone shapes. He sold his ice cream in the cones. The waffle cone was born.

In 1920, a young boy entered a store. The store was owned by Christian Nelson. The boy wanted a candy bar . . . or maybe an ice cream sandwich. He could not decide. Nelson wished he could sell the boy both things at once. He

invented an ice cream bar to please his candy and his ice cream customers at once. The Eskimo Pie® was born.

0-7696-3395-1 Inventions

Comprehension

Circle the best answer. Highlight the sentence or sentences in the story where you find your answer.

1. Before chewing gum was made commercially . . .
   a. no one had dreamed of chewing on something you did not swallow.
   b. people chewed on paper.
   c. people chewed on grasses, wax, leaves, and resin.
   d. people chewed on their fingers.

2. The first chewing-gum factory . . .
   a. was located in Europe.
   b. made gum from a chicle base.
   c. made gum from a spruce tree resin base.
   d. opened in 1748.

3. Thomas Adams . . .
   a. first manufactured gum with a chicle base.
   b. was a friend of John Curtis.
   c. was a friend of Black Jack.
   d. preached against chewing gum.

4. The first chicle-based gum was called . . .
   a. Wrigleys.
   b. White Queen.
   c. Bubblegum.
   d. Black Jack.

5. Gum did not begin to sell well until William Wrigley Jr. . . .
   a. sold it at his store.
   b. advertised it on radio.
   c. sent everyone in the phone book a sample piece.
   d. chewed 300 pieces at a state fair.

6. Ice cream sodas were invented . . .
   a. in the early 1700s.
   b. when a vendor ran out of flavorings for soda pops.
   c. on a cool day in San Francisco.
   d. on a Sunday.

7. Popsicles . . .
   a. are older than ice cream sodas.
   b. were invented by an old man.
   c. were born when soda water froze.
   d. were invented at a fair.

8. Ice cream sundaes . . .
   a. have soda water in them.
   b. are syrup-covered mounds of ice cream.
   c. were born in Maine.
   d. were named after their inventor.

9. Ernest Hamwi . . .
   a. sold crisp waffles to an ice cream vendor who ran out of bowls.
   b. ran out of ice cream at a fair in Louisiana.
   c. sold cotton candy at a fair.
   d. sold thick, soft waffles.

10. Christian Nelson . . .
   a. wanted an ice cream sandwich and a candy bar.
   b. sold ice cream out of a truck.
   c. invented the Eskimo Pie®.
   d. dipped ice cream in caramels.

Inventions by Chance: Chewing Gum and Ice Cream

Discussion Questions

1. In what ways were the ice cream inventions in this reading inventions of chance?

2. Chicle comes from the tropics. What other products come from tropical regions?

3. Could you live without ever snacking between meals? What are your favorite snacks? Would you miss ice cream or gum if you could never have either again?

Single Sentence Steps and Summaries

Divide the history of chewing gum into five single-sentence steps.

1. _____

2. _____

3. _____

4. _____

5. _____

Now summarize the story of one of the ice cream inventions from this story in a single sentence.

1. _____

Vocabulary Activities

Match the words on the right with their definitions on the left. Indicate your answers in the spaces provided.

_____	1. tree sap	a. ancient
_____	2. the region around the equator	b. carnival
_____	3. one who sells something	c. resin
_____	4. a fair	d. a plant
_____	5. very old	e. tropics
_____	6. a factory	f. scarce
_____	7. not readily available	g. vendor

Homework

Draw a picture of your favorite ice cream treat from the ones mentioned in the story. Write about its history below the picture.

Extension

Research and report on the history of your favorite food.

0-7696-3395-1 *Inventions*

Prereading Activities

Looking It Over

1. Read the title of the article that begins on page 76.

2. Leaf through the pages of the article, stopping to look at the pictures.

3. Read the list of vocabulary words.

What Do You Know?

How do you play basketball? Record here all the basketball rules you know.

_____

_____

_____

_____

_____

Make a Prediction

Why do you think someone invented basketball? How might the original rules have been different than they are today?

_____

_____

_____

_____

_____

Read the article to add to your knowledge.

Vocabulary

evolved   changed over time

Example: The scoring of basketball evolved over the years to include the three-point shot.

rituals   meaningful rites or practices common to a culture or religion

Example: Many Native American rituals include dance.

imitates   copies

Example: Chess imitates battlefield action.

suitable   appropriate

Example: A volleyball is not suitable for playing basketball since it does not dribble well.

adapt   change to fit the circumstances

Example: You can adapt the rules of many four-player games to suit partner play.

original   first

Example: The modern version of that song is not as good as the original.

Naismith Ball: The Birth of a New Sport

Few games have a real birthday. Most evolved out of dice, card, stick, and ball rituals. Even some that seem original are not. Chess imitates battlefield action. Volleyball is like an old game of hitting a ball into the air to see how long you will live.

Basketball is different. James Naismith made it unique. Unlike outdoor games, he made it suitable for indoor play. Unlike contact sports, it is free of tackling or tagging.

It all began in the winter of 1891. Boys at a school in Massachusetts were bored. Cold and snowy weather kept them from playing outdoor sports. So the school's physical education (p.e.) coach decided to make up a new indoor sport.

0-7696-3395-1 *Inventions*

Naismith did not know where to begin. Winter p.e. classes consisted of exercise workouts at that time. Naismith tried to adapt outdoor games for play in a gym. That did not work. He would have to come up with a new game. It would need to be playable in a small area. It could not result in falls on the hardwood floor of a gym.

Naismith had an idea. He asked the janitor to find two sturdy boxes. He would attach them to the balcony railings at either end of the gym. They would be goals. A soccer ball could be tossed into the boxes. "Box ball" may have been a big hit. But the janitor couldn't find sturdy boxes. Peach baskets would have to do.

The first game of basketball was awkward. Eighteen boys filled the court at once. No player could move more than one step when he had the ball. When a goal was made, a boy would have to climb a ladder to get the ball out of the basket. Sometimes the ball landed in the balcony. Then a boy would have to find the janitor. He was the only one with keys to the balcony.

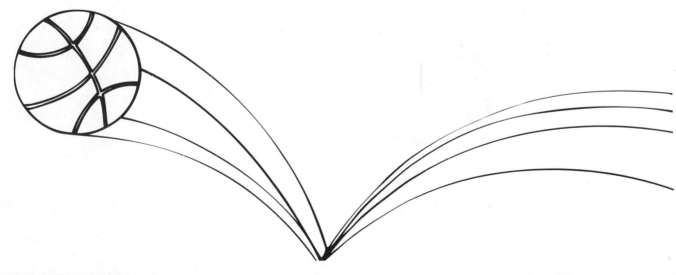

Slowly the game evolved. A hole was cut in the bottom of the peach baskets. Nets replaced peach baskets. New rules allowed players to dribble the ball. The game spread in popularity as it changed. Today, young kids and professional adults alike play basketball. In fact, it is now one of the most widely watched and played sports in the world.

0-7696-3395-1 *Inventions*

Comprehension

Circle the best answer. Highlight the sentence or sentences in the story where you find your answer.

1. Volleyball evolved out of . . .
   a. old dice and card games.
   b. an old ritual involving a stick and a ball.
   c. an old game of hitting a ball into the air to predict how long a person would live.
   d. battlefield games.

2. Basketball is unlike contact sports because . . .
   a. it is a single-player game.
   b. teams stay on their own sides of the court.
   c. the game involves no tagging or tackling.
   d. players tackle each other only at the end of halves.

3. Why did James Naismith invent a new indoor sport?
   a. He was tired of playing outdoor games.
   b. His children did not like playing in the snow.
   c. He could not adapt an outdoor game for indoor play.
   d. His wife asked him to create a game for their children to play indoors.

4. The first game of basketball . . .
   a. was played by girls.
   b. was played with peach baskets and a soccer ball.
   c. was played in Texas.
   d. lasted 18 minutes.

5. Which of the following was not an original basketball rule?
   a. Teams consisted of nine players.
   b. A player who had the ball could take only one step.
   c. Players could dribble the ball down the court.
   d. Goals were made when a ball landed in a basket.

What to Do with It: The Inventions of Jeans and Post-it® Notes · Clean It Off and Bandage It: The Inventions of Ivory® Soap and Band-Aids®

Nature Inspires: Teddy Bears and Velcro® Fasteners · By-Products of War: Silly Putty® and the Slinky® · Making Great Strides: Improvements in Doughnuts and Rubber

Zip and Chip: Step-by-Step Inventions · Inventions by Chance: Chewing Gum and Ice Cream · Naismith Ball: The Birth of a New Sport

Answer Key

What to Do with It ....pages 10–13

1. d	6. b
2. c	7. b
3. a	8. a
4. b	9. d
5. d	10. b

Step by Step: 1. Spence invents new glue. 3. Fry writes a note on a Post-it®. 5. 3M reps demonstrate the product. 6. 3M adds to its product line.

1. concocted	4. garments
2. generation	5. rivets
3. bolts	6. trousers

Clean It Off and Bandage It........pages 20–23

1. b	6. b
2. b	7. c
3. c	8. d
4. c	9. b
5. a	10. a

Create a Timeline: 3000 B.C., Cleansers are mentioned in the Bible. A.D. 100, Soap dyes are referred to in writings. 1878, Bathing is in vogue. 1879, Ivory is first sold. 1891, "It floats" becomes an Ivory slogan.

1. paint	5. chocolate
2. remember	6. injury
3. wallpaper	7. lazy
4. unpopular	

Nature Inspires ....pages 30–33

1. c	6. a
2. a	7. b
3. c	8. a
4. d	9. b
5. c	10. c

Prove It! 1. As he did, he thought of a question. What made burs stick so well? de Mestral looked at a corner of his coat under a microscope. 2. He often went on hikes. He also liked to swim and jog. On this trip, he wanted to hunt. 3. He saw that hooks on burs engaged in loops on fabric. This gave de Mestral an idea. Strips of hooks could be attached to strips of loops.

By-Products of War ....pages 40–43

1. d	6. d
2. a	7. b
3. c	8. d
4. a	9. a
5. c	10. d

1. antonyms	4. antonyms
2. synonyms	5. synonyms
3. synonyms	

Making Great Strides ....pages 50–53

1. d	6. d
2. a	7. b
3. c	8. d
4. d	9. b
5. a	10. c

The Doughnut Game: 1. d = length across doughnut; 2. yeast; 3. 1/2 length across doughnut hole; 4. true; 5. $a = 3.14r^2$; 6. 5/8; 7. 63%; 8. false

1. dedicate	5. valve
2. brittle	6. indebted
3. absorb	7. institution
4. enlist	

Zip and Chip ....pages 60–63

1. d	6. b
2. c	7. a
3. d	8. a
4. b	9. b
5. d	10. c

Identifying Fasteners: 1. shoestrings; 2. snaps; 3. belt; 4. buttons; 5. zipper; 6. hook and loop fasteners

1. locals	4. sport
2. device	5. region
3. industry	6. remodeled

Inventions by Chance ....pages 70–73

1. c	6. b
2. c	7. c
3. a	8. b
4. d	9. a
5. c	10. c

Single Sentence Steps and Summaries: 1. People chewed grasses and wax. 2. John Curtis opened the first gum factory. 3. Thomas Adams began making gum with chicle. 4. Some people preached against chewing gum. 5. Wrigley popularized gum by sending one piece to everyone in the phone book. Sentences about ice cream inventions will vary.

1. c	5. a
2. e	6. d
3. g	7. f
4. b	

Naismith Ball ....page 79

1. c	4. b
2. c	5. c
3. c	